Troubleshooting and Operating Systems

Mastering PC Troubleshooting and Operating Systems

The Future-Ready Guide for 2025 AND BEYOND

Second Edition: 2025

MARK JOHN LADO

DEDICATION

To the problem solvers, innovators, and lifelong learners who embrace the ever-changing world of technology—this book is for you.

The world of PC troubleshooting and operating systems is evolving at an unprecedented pace, and it takes curiosity, persistence, and adaptability to stay ahead. Whether you're an IT professional, a student, a tech enthusiast, or someone who simply loves to understand how computers work, your passion for learning drives technological progress.

I dedicate this book to educators who inspire the next generation of tech experts, IT professionals who keep systems running smoothly, and enthusiasts who never stop asking "why" and "how." Your dedication to mastering complex systems ensures that the digital world remains reliable, efficient, and secure.

To my family and friends—your unwavering support fuels my passion for writing and teaching. Your belief in my work motivates me to continue exploring and sharing knowledge.

May this book empower you with the skills, confidence, and insights to tackle any technical challenge that comes your way.

ACKNOWLEDGMENTS

Writing this book was both a challenging and rewarding journey, and I am deeply grateful to those who supported me along the way.

First and foremost, thank you to my family and friends for your encouragement and patience. Your unwavering support gave me the motivation to complete this project.

To my colleagues and mentors in the IT industry, your insights and discussions about emerging technologies played a crucial role in shaping the depth of this book. Your expertise in hardware, operating systems, AI, cybersecurity, and networking helped refine the topics covered.

A special thanks to tech educators and students, whose curiosity and enthusiasm continue to push the boundaries of learning. Your passion for understanding and improving technology is what drives innovation.

Finally, to the readers—whether you are a beginner or an experienced IT professional—thank you for trusting this book as a guide to mastering PC troubleshooting and operating systems. I hope it equips you with practical knowledge and future-ready skills to navigate the ever-evolving tech landscape.

Your commitment to learning is what keeps technology advancing.
Thank you!

Table of Contents

Introduction

In an age where technology underpins nearly every aspect of daily life, understanding how to effectively troubleshoot and optimize personal computers is more critical than ever. The COVID-19 pandemic accelerated the global shift toward remote work, digital education, and online services, underscoring the importance of reliable and efficient PC systems.

This book, Mastering PC Troubleshooting and Operating Systems: The Future-Ready Guide for 2025, is designed to equip readers with the tools, techniques, and knowledge required to navigate the complexities of modern computing environments. From understanding the evolution of PC troubleshooting to leveraging artificial intelligence, quantum computing, and sustainable hardware innovations, this guide covers it all.

Whether you are a tech enthusiast, a professional IT technician, or a curious learner, this book will provide practical insights and real-world examples to empower you in mastering the art of PC troubleshooting. Let's dive into the future of technology together.

Chapter 1

The Evolution of PC Troubleshooting in the 2020s

In an era defined by rapid technological advancement, the role of PC troubleshooting has become more pivotal than ever. Chapter 1 delves into the fascinating evolution of troubleshooting practices, tracing the journey from manual, hardware-centric diagnostics of the past to the sophisticated, AI-driven solutions of today. By exploring historical trends, the impact of the post-pandemic digital shift, and the transformative power of artificial intelligence, this chapter sets the stage for understanding how troubleshooting has adapted to meet the demands of increasingly complex and interconnected systems.

History and Trends in PC Troubleshooting

PC troubleshooting has evolved significantly over the decades. In the early days of personal computing, troubleshooting was primarily manual and limited to a niche group of tech-savvy individuals. Early computers like the IBM PC required users to understand basic electronics and programming to diagnose hardware or software issues. For example, identifying faulty RAM or a misaligned disk drive often involved using tools like oscilloscopes or command-line diagnostics.

The 2000s saw the rise of graphical operating systems and more intuitive user interfaces, simplifying troubleshooting for everyday users. Tools like Windows System Restore and macOS's Disk Utility emerged to make diagnostics and repairs more accessible. The introduction of online support communities, such as forums and technical blogs, created a collaborative environment for problem-solving.

In the 2020s, trends in PC troubleshooting reflect the increasing complexity of computing systems. Multi-core processors, cloud-based storage, and hybrid software ecosystems have introduced new challenges. However, advanced diagnostic tools like built-in self-repair features, predictive analytics, and detailed error logs have also empowered users to identify and address issues with minimal external assistance.

Real-World Example:

A clear example of modern troubleshooting evolution is the inclusion of Microsoft's "Troubleshoot" feature in Windows 11. It allows users to automatically diagnose and fix common issues like network connectivity or printer malfunctions by leveraging built-in AI algorithms.

Importance of Troubleshooting in a Post-Pandemic Digital World

The COVID-19 pandemic accelerated the global shift toward remote work, digital learning, and online services, underscoring the critical importance of reliable PC systems. Downtime caused by PC issues now has immediate consequences, such as missed virtual meetings, disrupted online learning sessions, or delayed e-commerce transactions.

Key Factors:

Increased Dependency on PCs: With many professionals and students working and studying from home, PCs became central to daily life.

Diverse Use Cases: From video conferencing tools like Zoom and Teams to collaborative platforms like Slack, troubleshooting often involves diagnosing software compatibility and bandwidth-related issues.

Cybersecurity Threats: The rise in cyberattacks, including phishing and ransomware, made robust security troubleshooting an essential skill.

Real-World Example:

Consider the case of small businesses during the pandemic. Many had to adapt quickly by enabling remote access to office PCs. Troubleshooting VPN connections, resolving latency issues, and securing remote desktops became pivotal for ensuring business continuity. IT professionals were tasked with deploying robust solutions like remote monitoring tools (e.g., TeamViewer) and training employees in basic troubleshooting.

Role of Artificial Intelligence in Diagnostic Tools

Artificial Intelligence (AI) has revolutionized PC troubleshooting, making it faster, more accurate, and predictive. AI-driven diagnostic tools analyze vast datasets to identify patterns, predict failures, and suggest solutions.

Key Features of AI in Troubleshooting:

Predictive Maintenance: AI can analyze system logs and hardware telemetry to forecast potential failures. For example, tools like CrystalDiskInfo use machine learning to predict hard drive failures based on SMART (Self-Monitoring, Analysis, and Reporting Technology) data.

Automated Diagnostics: Tools like Microsoft's Windows Defender leverage AI to detect malware and other security threats in real time, minimizing the need for manual intervention.

Virtual Assistants: AI-driven assistants such as Apple's Siri or Google Assistant offer step-by-step guides to resolve basic issues, enhancing user self-sufficiency.

Real-World Example:

Dell's SupportAssist is an excellent illustration of AI in action. It proactively monitors PCs for hardware or software issues and provides automated resolutions. For instance, if a user's system is running low on memory, Support Assist alerts them and guides them through freeing up space or upgrading hardware components.

Conclusion

The evolution of PC troubleshooting reflects the growing complexity and centrality of technology in daily life. From the early manual methods to today's AI-driven diagnostics, the field has continuously adapted to meet the demands of users. In a post-pandemic world, the ability to quickly and effectively troubleshoot PCs is more critical than ever. With AI leading the way, the future of PC troubleshooting promises even greater efficiency, accessibility, and resilience against emerging challenges.

Comprehensive Test Assessment for Chapter 1

Test I: Multiple-Choice Questions

Instructions: Read each question carefully. Select the correct answer by encircling the letter of your choice.

1. Which tool was commonly used for manual troubleshooting in the early days of PC computing?

   A. Microsoft Defender

   B. Oscilloscope

   C. Windows System Restore

   D. AI Virtual Assistant

2. What feature in Windows 11 automates common troubleshooting tasks?

   A. CrystalDiskInfo

   B. Task Manager

   C. Troubleshoot

   D. UEFI Interface

3. During the 2000s, which of the following simplified troubleshooting for everyday users?

   A. Command-line diagnostics

   B. Multi-core processors

   C. Graphical operating systems

   D. AI predictive analytics

4. What key challenge did the 2020s introduce to PC troubleshooting?

   A. Limited user interfaces

B. Basic hardware systems

C. Cloud-based storage and hybrid ecosystems

D. Manual troubleshooting

5. AI-driven assistants like Siri and Google Assistant enhance troubleshooting by:

A. Predicting failures using system logs

B. Offering step-by-step guidance to resolve issues

C. Detecting malware in real time

D. Monitoring hardware components proactively

6. Why was PC troubleshooting critical in the post-pandemic digital world?

A. To improve video game performance

B. To diagnose faulty electronics

C. To ensure uninterrupted virtual work and learning

D. To enhance entertainment streaming quality

7. What is a core capability of AI in troubleshooting?

A. Superposition analysis

B. Predictive maintenance

C. Network encryption

D. Application partitioning

8. Which tool uses machine learning to predict hard drive failures?

A. Microsoft Teams

B. CrystalDiskInfo

C. Dell's SupportAssist

D. Wireshark

9. What does zero-trust security architecture assume?

A. All devices and users are inherently trustworthy

B. All devices and users must verify their credentials

C. Only corporate-owned devices need verification

D. Users are automatically granted access

10. The introduction of AI in troubleshooting primarily aims to:

    A. Make manual diagnostics easier

    B. Prevent cyberattacks altogether

    C. Automate and enhance issue resolution

    D. Replace hardware entirely

Test II: Identification

Instructions: Identify the term or concept being described. Write your answer in the space provided.

1. A technology that enables the proactive detection of system failures using AI and hardware telemetry.

2. A feature in Windows 11 that diagnoses and resolves common PC issues automatically.

3. A diagnostic method that was common during the early era of computing, requiring basic programming knowledge.

4. The global event that accelerated the need for robust troubleshooting skills in the 2020s.

5. An AI-driven tool by Dell that monitors and resolves PC issues autonomously.

6. A hardware issue in early PCs that required oscilloscopes for detection.

7. The type of operating systems introduced in the 2000s that improved user accessibility for troubleshooting.

8. A collaborative environment for solving PC problems introduced through online forums and blogs.

9. The key security challenge that surged during the post-pandemic era.

10. The process of analyzing redundant files and optimizing storage using AI tools.

Test III: True-or-False Questions

Instructions: Read each statement carefully. Write T if the statement is true and F if it is false.

1. AI in troubleshooting reduces the need for manual diagnostics.
2. Virtual assistants like Siri and Google Assistant cannot resolve basic PC issues.
3. The introduction of graphical operating systems in the 2000s made troubleshooting less accessible.
4. Multi-core processors and cloud-based storage simplified PC troubleshooting in the 2020s.
5. Troubleshooting was critical during the COVID-19 pandemic due to increased dependency on PCs.
6. Predictive maintenance uses system logs to forecast potential hardware failures.
7. Dell's SupportAssist alerts users about memory issues and provides solutions.
8. Oscilloscopes are still widely used for troubleshooting in modern PCs.
9. Online forums and blogs contributed to collaborative troubleshooting efforts in the 2000s.
10. AI has no significant impact on modern PC troubleshooting methods.

Test IV: Matching-Type Questions

Instructions: Match the items in Column A with their corresponding descriptions in Column B. Write the letter of the correct match on the blank provided.

Column A

1. Predictive Maintenance
2. Windows System Restore
3. Multi-core Processors
4. Zero-Trust Security
5. Graphical Operating Systems
6. Troubleshoot Feature in Windows 11
7. CrystalDiskInfo
8. AI Diagnostic Tools
9. Online Support Communities
10. COVID-19 Pandemic

Column B

A. A tool designed to predict hard drive failures using machine learning.

B. Diagnoses and resolves issues automatically in modern Windows OS.

C. Accelerated dependency on troubleshooting for remote work and education.

D. Simplifies troubleshooting by providing an intuitive user interface.

E. Assumes no device or user is inherently trustworthy.

F. A feature that allows users to restore their system to a previous state.

G. Enhanced computing capabilities but introduced new troubleshooting challenges.

H. An AI-driven capability that identifies anomalies and suggests solutions.

I. Provides collaborative solutions through forums and technical blogs.

J. Analyzes system logs to forecast hardware issues.

Test V: Essay Question

Instructions: Write a concise and well-organized essay on the following topic. Provide specific examples to support your answer.

Question:
How has the evolution of PC troubleshooting from manual methods to AI-driven diagnostics impacted user accessibility and efficiency in resolving PC issues? Include real-world examples discussed in the chapter.

Chapter 2

Hardware Innovations Shaping 2025

Chapter 2 explores the groundbreaking advancements in hardware technology that are shaping the landscape of computing in 2025. From next-generation CPUs and GPUs that deliver unprecedented power and efficiency to the transformative potential of quantum computing, this chapter provides a comprehensive look at the technologies driving innovation. It also highlights the critical role of cutting-edge SSDs in supporting data-intensive tasks and examines the industry's commitment to sustainability through eco-friendly designs and practices. With real-world examples and practical insights, this chapter underscores how these hardware innovations are redefining performance, productivity, and environmental responsibility in modern computing.

Overview of Next-Generation CPUs and GPUs

As technology progresses, CPUs and GPUs continue to evolve, offering unprecedented performance and efficiency. The CPUs of 2025 are expected to feature more cores, improved power efficiency, and enhanced AI processing capabilities. For instance, AMD's Zen 5 and Intel's Meteor Lake architectures are projected to redefine computational efficiency with AI integration directly on the chip.

On the GPU front, innovations like NVIDIA's Ada Lovelace and AMD's RDNA 4 architectures deliver real-time ray tracing, improved tensor core performance, and superior energy efficiency. These GPUs cater not only to gaming enthusiasts but also to professionals in AI, machine learning, and 3D rendering.

Real-World Example:

NVIDIA's RTX 5000 series demonstrates how AI-enhanced GPUs accelerate workflows, such as real-time video editing, scientific simulations, and AI-driven image recognition.

Quantum Computing Basics for Enthusiasts

Quantum computing represents a paradigm shift in computational power, leveraging quantum bits (qubits) to perform complex calculations exponentially faster than classical computers. While still in its nascent stage for consumer markets, companies like IBM and Google are making quantum computing accessible through cloud platforms.

Key Concepts:

Superposition: Qubits can represent multiple states simultaneously, enabling massive parallel computations.

Entanglement: Quantum particles become interconnected, allowing instantaneous data transfer over distances.

Applications: Cryptography, optimization problems, and simulations in physics and chemistry.

Real-World Example:

IBM's Quantum Experience platform allows enthusiasts to experiment with quantum algorithms, providing a gateway into this futuristic technology.

Advances in SSD Technology: NVMe 5.0

Storage technology has seen a significant leap with the introduction of NVMe 5.0 SSDs. These drives offer blistering speeds of up to 14 GB/s, reducing bottlenecks in data-intensive applications like 8K video editing and large-scale simulations. The lower latency and enhanced durability of NVMe 5.0 make it a critical component for high-performance PCs.

Real-World Example:

Content creators using NVMe 5.0 SSDs can edit high-resolution videos directly from the drive without experiencing lag, streamlining their workflows and boosting productivity.

Sustainable and Eco-Friendly PC Components

The tech industry is increasingly focusing on sustainability, producing eco-friendly components to reduce electronic waste and energy consumption. Manufacturers are using recyclable materials, improving power efficiency, and implementing modular designs for easier upgrades.

Key Innovations:

Eco-Friendly Packaging: Companies like Dell and HP are utilizing biodegradable packaging.

Low-Power Components: ARM-based processors are leading the charge in energy-efficient computing.

Modular Designs: Framework laptops allow users to upgrade individual components, extending device lifespans.

Real-World Example:

The Framework Laptop exemplifies sustainability by enabling users to replace or upgrade parts like RAM, SSDs, and even motherboards, significantly reducing e-waste.

Conclusion

Hardware innovations in 2025 highlight the relentless pace of technological advancement. From next-generation processors and quantum computing to cutting-edge SSDs and sustainable components, the future of hardware promises enhanced performance, efficiency, and environmental responsibility. As these innovations become mainstream, they will redefine how users interact with and rely on their PCs.

Comprehensive Test Assessment for Chapter 2

Test I: Multiple-Choice Questions

Instructions: Read each question carefully. Select the correct answer by encircling the letter of your choice.

1. What is a key feature of next-generation CPUs in 2025?

   A. Fewer cores with higher clock speeds

   B. Enhanced AI processing capabilities

   C. Reduced power consumption but slower performance

   D. Lack of compatibility with hybrid software ecosystems

2. Which GPU architecture is known for delivering real-time ray tracing and energy efficiency?

   A. AMD Zen 5

   B. NVIDIA Ada Lovelace

   C. Intel Meteor Lake

   D. ARM Cortex-A78

3. Quantum computing uses qubits to achieve:

   A. Improved heat dissipation

   B. Massive parallel computations through superposition

   C. Compatibility with NVMe 5.0 SSDs

   D. Incremental hardware updates

4. What speeds can NVMe 5.0 SSDs achieve?

   A. Up to 10 GB/s

   B. Up to 14 GB/s

   C. Up to 8 GB/s

   D. Up to 12 GB/s

5. What is the purpose of ARM-based processors in modern computing?

   A. Enhancing gaming performance through ray tracing

   B. Increasing energy efficiency in computing

   C. Enabling qubit-based operations for quantum computing

   D. Supporting modular designs for easier upgrades

6. Which platform provides enthusiasts with access to quantum computing experimentation?

   A. NVIDIA GeForce Experience

   B. IBM's Quantum Experience

   C. VMware Workstation

   D. Google Cloud AI

7. What sustainability innovation is exemplified by Framework laptops?

   A. High-speed NVMe 5.0 SSDs

   B. Biodegradable packaging for components

   C. Modular designs for easy part replacement and upgrades

   D. AI-driven energy management systems

8. Which industry application benefits most from quantum computing?

   A. Real-time video editing

   B. Cryptography and optimization problems

   C. High-speed gaming

   D. Content creation workflows

9. Which innovation allows creators to edit high-resolution videos without lag?

   A. NVIDIA Ada Lovelace GPUs

   B. ARM-based processors

C. NVMe 5.0 SSDs

D. AMD Zen 5 CPUs

10. What is the primary environmental benefit of eco-friendly PC components?

A. Increased storage capacity

B. Reduced e-waste and energy consumption

C. Higher processing speeds

D. Improved cloud compatibility

Test II: Identification

Instructions: Identify the term or concept being described. Write your answer in the space provided.

1. The GPU architecture known for real-time ray tracing and superior energy efficiency.

2. The key quantum computing principle that allows qubits to represent multiple states simultaneously.

3. A storage technology capable of speeds up to 14 GB/s, used in high-performance PCs.

4. A platform offering users the opportunity to experiment with quantum algorithms.

5. A modular laptop design that allows easy replacement and upgrades of components.

6. A 2025 CPU architecture integrating AI capabilities directly onto the chip.

7. A sustainability initiative involving the use of biodegradable packaging by tech companies.

8. The property of quantum particles that allows instantaneous data transfer over distances.

9. A processor type leading the charge in energy-efficient computing.

10. An SSD feature that significantly reduces bottlenecks in data-intensive applications.

Test III: True-or-False Questions

Instructions: Read each statement carefully. Write T if the statement is true and F if it is false.

1. NVMe 5.0 SSDs have speeds lower than 10 GB/s.
2. Quantum computing is widely available in consumer devices in 2025.
3. NVIDIA's RTX 5000 series GPUs are optimized for AI-driven workflows.
4. Modular designs in laptops increase electronic waste.
5. IBM's Quantum Experience is a platform for quantum computing experimentation.
6. AMD's Zen 5 CPUs are designed to enhance AI performance.
7. ARM-based processors are known for their high energy consumption.
8. Sustainable PC components include designs that allow easy upgrades.
9. Superposition enables qubits to perform multiple computations simultaneously.

10. Quantum computing has significant applications in cryptography and simulations.

Test IV: Matching-Type Questions

Instructions: Match the items in Column A with their corresponding descriptions in Column B. Write the letter of the correct match on the blank provided.

Column A

1. NVIDIA Ada Lovelace
2. Quantum Superposition
3. NVMe 5.0 SSD
4. Framework Laptop
5. IBM's Quantum Experience
6. AMD Zen 5
7. Modular Designs
8. ARM-Based Processors
9. Real-Time Ray Tracing
10. Sustainable Packaging

Column B

A. Allows users to upgrade parts, reducing e-waste.

B. Provides experimentation access to quantum computing.

C. A GPU innovation delivering high-quality lighting effects in games.

D. Significantly boosts storage performance with speeds up to 14 GB/s.

E. A feature of quantum particles enabling parallel computations.

F. Designed for energy-efficient computing.

G. Enhances AI processing on CPUs.

H. A laptop known for sustainability and part replacement ease.

I. A GPU architecture enabling AI-enhanced workflows.

J. Reduces environmental impact through biodegradable materials.

Test V: Essay Question

Instructions: Write a concise and well-organized essay on the following topic. Provide specific examples to support your answer.

Question:
How are hardware innovations such as next-generation CPUs, GPUs, and sustainable components shaping the future of computing in 2025? Discuss their impact on performance, productivity, and environmental responsibility.

Chapter 3

Operating Systems in 2025

Chapter 3 delves into the dynamic world of operating systems in 2025, spotlighting the innovations that enhance user experience, security, and performance. From the AI-driven capabilities of Windows 12 and macOS Next's seamless integration within the Apple ecosystem to Linux's advances in real-time processing and containerization, this chapter captures the diversity and adaptability of modern OS platforms. It also explores the growing role of open-source systems in education and startups and highlights how artificial intelligence is reshaping functionality and user productivity. With practical examples and forward-looking insights, this chapter showcases the critical role operating systems play in shaping the future of computing.

Major OS Updates: Windows 12, macOS Next, and Kernel Innovations in Linux

The operating systems landscape in 2025 is marked by significant updates that enhance user experience, security, and performance. Windows 12 introduces a more AI-centric approach, leveraging tools like Copilot to provide contextual assistance and automate repetitive tasks. Additionally, its modular architecture ensures optimized performance for a wide range of devices, from gaming PCs to lightweight laptops.

macOS Next focuses on seamless integration within Apple's ecosystem. Features like advanced handoff capabilities between devices and improved AR support reflect Apple's commitment to user-centric design. Meanwhile, Linux kernels have embraced real-time processing and enhanced containerization, making the open-source OS a formidable choice for developers and enterprises alike.

Real-World Example:

Canonical's Ubuntu 25.04 exemplifies Linux's role in enterprise computing by offering robust support for Kubernetes and AI workloads.

Role of Open-Source OS in Education and Startups

Open-source operating systems continue to democratize technology by offering free and customizable platforms. In education, Linux distributions like Ubuntu and Fedora are invaluable for teaching programming, server management, and cybersecurity. Startups benefit from the cost savings and flexibility of open-source OS, which enable them to scale their IT infrastructure efficiently.

Real-World Example:

A nonprofit coding bootcamp in Kenya utilizes Linux-based systems to teach students programming, significantly reducing costs while providing hands-on experience with industry-relevant tools.

Integration of AI in Modern Operating Systems

Modern operating systems increasingly rely on AI to enhance functionality and user experience. AI-driven features include predictive file search, automated system optimization, and personalized recommendations. For example, Windows 12's AI-powered task manager dynamically reallocates resources to ensure optimal performance during high-demand applications.

macOS incorporates AI for advanced photo and video editing tools, while Linux leverages machine learning for efficient system monitoring in server environments.

Real-World Example:

Windows 12's Copilot uses AI to streamline workflows by suggesting shortcuts and automating multi-step tasks, improving productivity for both casual and professional users.

Conclusion

Operating systems in 2025 embody a synergy of AI, user-centric design, and open-source innovation. These advancements ensure that OS platforms remain adaptable to the needs of diverse user groups, from individual consumers to global enterprises. By leveraging AI and fostering accessibility, operating systems continue to shape the future of computing.

Comprehensive Test Assessment for Chapter 3

Test I: Multiple-Choice Questions

Instructions: Read each question carefully. Select the correct answer by encircling the letter of your choice.

1. What is a key feature of Windows 12 in 2025?

    A. Real-time ray tracing

    B. Copilot for AI-driven contextual assistance

    C. Modular components for sustainability

    D. Blockchain-powered security

2. Which operating system focuses on seamless integration within the Apple ecosystem?

    A. Ubuntu 25.04

    B. macOS Next

    C. Windows 12

    D. Fedora

3. What improvement is a hallmark of Linux kernels in 2025?

    A. Advanced AR integration

    B. AI-powered Copilot

    C. Enhanced containerization and real-time processing

    D. Seamless Handoff between devices

4. How do open-source operating systems benefit startups?

    A. By offering pre-installed proprietary software

    B. By providing cost-effective and scalable IT infrastructure

    C. By eliminating the need for cybersecurity

    D. By limiting access to programming tools

5. What AI feature does Windows 12's task manager offer?

   A. Resource reallocation during high-demand applications

   B. Real-time malware scanning

   C. Predictive search for programming files

   D. Automated cloud storage backups

6. Which operating system version supports Kubernetes and AI workloads?

   A. Windows 12

   B. macOS Next

   C. Canonical's Ubuntu 25.04

   D. Fedora 40.12

7. What technology enhances macOS Next's user experience?

   A. Blockchain authentication

   B. AR support and advanced handoff capabilities

   C. Predictive maintenance tools

   D. Virtual reality troubleshooting

8. What is an example of AI integration in Linux operating systems?

   A. Advanced AR editing tools

   B. Automated network configuration

   C. Machine learning for efficient system monitoring

   D. AI-powered task automation

9. How are Linux-based systems used in education?

   A. To teach gaming development exclusively

   B. To simulate blockchain environments

   C. To teach programming, server management, and cybersecurity

   D. To reduce the need for IT infrastructure

10. What is a primary goal of AI in modern operating systems?

    A. To replace human intervention entirely

    B. To enhance functionality and user productivity

    C. To eliminate proprietary software usage

    D. To focus exclusively on cybersecurity

Test II: Identification

Instructions: Identify the term or concept being described. Write your answer in the space provided.

1. The AI-driven tool in Windows 12 that automates tasks and provides contextual assistance.

2. An operating system that offers real-time processing and supports Kubernetes.

3. A Linux-based distribution used in education to teach programming and cybersecurity.

4. The feature in macOS Next that allows seamless communication between devices.

5. A nonprofit that uses Linux-based systems to reduce costs in coding bootcamps.

6. The integration of AI in macOS for advanced multimedia editing.

7. The technology in Linux that enhances resource allocation in server environments.

8. An operating system that scales IT infrastructure cost-effectively for startups.

9. The task manager feature in Windows 12 that optimizes system performance.

10. An innovation in Linux kernels that enhances the management of software containers.

Test III: True-or-False Questions

Instructions: Read each statement carefully. Write T if the statement is true and F if it is false.

1. Windows 12 introduces AR integration for seamless device communication.
2. Open-source operating systems are less suitable for startups due to high costs.
3. Ubuntu 25.04 supports AI workloads and Kubernetes for enterprise use.
4. AI in operating systems helps optimize system performance automatically.
5. macOS Next focuses on real-time processing for AI workloads.
6. Open-source operating systems are widely used for teaching programming and cybersecurity.
7. Linux operating systems in 2025 rely on proprietary software for containerization.
8. Windows 12's AI-powered task manager enhances user productivity during high-demand tasks.
9. macOS Next supports advanced handoff features and AR capabilities.
10. AI features in modern operating systems improve both functionality and user experience.

Test IV: Matching-Type Questions

Instructions: Match the items in Column A with their corresponding descriptions in Column B. Write the letter of the correct match on the blank provided.

Column A

1. Windows 12 Copilot
2. Ubuntu 25.04
3. macOS Next
4. AI in Linux
5. Handoff Features
6. Open-Source OS
7. Containerization
8. AI-Powered Task Manager
9. Programming Bootcamps
10. Modular Architecture

Column B

A. Seamlessly transfers tasks between Apple devices.

B. Automates repetitive tasks and enhances productivity.

C. Offers robust support for Kubernetes and AI workloads.

D. A key innovation in Linux for managing software environments.

E. Uses Linux systems to teach cybersecurity and server management.

F. Enhances user productivity during high-demand applications.

G. Designed to optimize performance across multiple device types.

H. Ensures efficient system monitoring using machine learning.

I. A cost-effective IT solution for startups and educational institutions.

J. Supports AR tools and seamless integration in the Apple ecosystem.

Test V: Essay Question

Instructions: Write a concise and well-organized essay on the following topic. Provide specific examples to support your answer.

Question:
How do the advancements in Windows 12, macOS Next, and Linux operating systems enhance user experience, security, and productivity in 2025? Provide real-world examples to illustrate their impact.

Chapter 4

Setting Up and Optimizing Smart Workstations

Chapter 4 focuses on the tools and strategies essential for setting up and optimizing smart workstations in 2025. From leveraging advanced BIOS and UEFI configurations for enhanced performance and security to managing multi-boot systems for diverse operating system needs, this chapter provides a comprehensive guide for maximizing workstation efficiency. Additionally, it highlights the power of cloud-connected PCs in fostering seamless collaboration and productivity across devices. Through real-world examples and actionable insights, this chapter equips users with the knowledge to create workstations that meet the demands of modern digital environments.

Smart BIOS and UEFI Configurations

Modern BIOS and UEFI systems offer advanced configuration options that enhance performance and security. Features like fast boot, hardware diagnostics, and AI-powered settings adjustments allow users to optimize their systems for specific workloads.

Real-World Example:

The ASUS ROG UEFI interface includes AI Overclocking, which

monitors system performance and adjusts settings automatically to achieve optimal CPU performance without risking stability.

Installing and Managing Multi-Boot Systems with Ease

Multi-boot setups are invaluable for users needing access to multiple operating systems. With tools like GRUB (for Linux) or macOS Boot Camp, users can efficiently manage different OS environments. Key considerations include proper partitioning and using a reliable boot loader.

Real-World Example:

A software developer dual-boots Windows 12 for gaming and Ubuntu for development, leveraging each OS's strengths to maximize productivity and performance.

Cloud-Connected PCs: Syncing with Modern Cloud Services

Cloud-connected PCs streamline workflows by integrating storage and software across devices. Services like Microsoft OneDrive, Google Drive, and iCloud allow seamless file syncing, remote access, and enhanced collaboration.

Real-World Example:

An architect working on a collaborative project uses Autodesk's cloud integration to share CAD files in real time with team members across different locations.

Conclusion

Optimizing smart workstations in 2025 involves leveraging advanced BIOS/UEFI configurations, managing multi-boot systems effectively, and fully utilizing cloud connectivity. These innovations ensure enhanced productivity, flexibility, and seamless collaboration in increasingly digital work environments.

Comprehensive Test Assessment for Chapter 4

Test I: Multiple-Choice Questions

Instructions: Read each question carefully. Select the correct answer by encircling the letter of your choice.

1. What feature in modern BIOS/UEFI systems helps optimize system performance?

   A. AI-powered Overclocking

   B. Multi-boot partitioning

   C. Cloud storage integration

   D. Compatibility layers

2. Which tool allows for efficient management of multiple operating systems?

   A. Microsoft OneDrive

   B. GRUB for Linux

   C. ASUS AI Diagnostics

   D. Autodesk CAD

3. What is a key consideration when setting up a multi-boot system?

   A. Installing cloud-connected software

   B. Proper partitioning and boot loader selection

   C. Disabling UEFI features

   D. Maximizing GPU overclocking

4. Which cloud service is commonly used for file syncing and collaboration?

   A. NVIDIA GeForce Now

B. VMware Workstation

C. Google Drive

D. ASUS ROG Interface

5. What is the benefit of using AI-powered BIOS/UEFI settings?

A. Automatic system upgrades

B. Enhanced CPU performance without compromising stability

C. Increased compatibility for multi-boot systems

D. Seamless integration with cloud services

6. What does the ASUS ROG UEFI interface provide?

A. Real-time ray tracing adjustments

B. AI Overclocking for optimized CPU performance

C. Compatibility with quantum computing

D. Advanced software virtualization tools

7. How do cloud-connected PCs enhance productivity?

A. By reducing hardware requirements

B. By syncing storage and software across devices

C. By enabling dual-boot functionality

D. By automating hardware configurations

8. What tool does macOS provide for multi-boot system management?

A. Boot Manager

B. GRUB

C. Boot Camp

D. Ubuntu Loader

9. What role do cloud services play in collaborative projects?

A. Increasing hardware compatibility

B. Sharing files in real time across team members

C. Automating BIOS configurations

D. Enhancing GPU rendering capabilities

10. Which of the following is NOT a feature of smart BIOS/UEFI systems?

A. Fast boot

B. AI-powered settings adjustments

C. Multi-device syncing

D. Hardware diagnostics

Test II: Identification

Instructions: Identify the term or concept being described. Write your answer in the space provided.

1. A feature in BIOS/UEFI systems that monitors performance and adjusts settings automatically.

2. A tool that enables multi-boot setups on Linux-based systems.

3. The type of systems that sync storage and software across devices for enhanced productivity.

4. The cloud service used by architects to collaborate on CAD files in real time.

5. A critical factor in setting up multi-boot systems to avoid conflicts.

6. A UEFI interface feature that ensures optimal CPU performance without risking stability.

7. The macOS tool for managing multiple operating systems on a single device.

8. The type of project where cloud integration enhances real-time collaboration.

9. The service that allows seamless syncing of files across multiple devices and users.

10. A configuration system that provides advanced options for optimizing performance and security.

Test III: True-or-False Questions

Instructions: Read each statement carefully. Write T if the statement is true and F if it is false.

1. AI-powered overclocking in BIOS/UEFI settings ensures stability while optimizing performance.
2. Multi-boot setups do not require partitioning or a reliable boot loader.
3. Cloud-connected PCs are primarily used for gaming.
4. Autodesk's cloud integration is useful for collaborative architectural projects.
5. GRUB is a tool used for managing multi-boot systems on Linux.
6. Advanced BIOS/UEFI configurations include features like hardware diagnostics and fast boot.
7. macOS Boot Camp is used to set up and manage multi-boot systems.
8. Cloud services eliminate the need for multi-boot setups.
9. BIOS/UEFI configurations can enhance workstation security.
10. Cloud-connected PCs can integrate storage and software across devices.

Test IV: Matching-Type Questions

Instructions: Match the items in Column A with their corresponding descriptions in Column B. Write the letter of the correct match on the blank provided.

Column A

1. AI Overclocking
2. GRUB
3. Cloud-Connected PC
4. Boot Camp
5. Google Drive
6. UEFI Interface
7. Partitioning
8. Autodesk Cloud Integration
9. ASUS ROG Interface
10. Fast Boot

Column B

A. A cloud service for file syncing and collaboration.

B. A macOS tool for managing multiple operating systems.

C. Adjusts CPU settings automatically for optimal performance.

D. Ensures faster startup times in modern systems.

E. A Linux tool for managing multi-boot setups.

F. Provides real-time collaboration for CAD files.

G. Syncs storage and software across devices for seamless productivity.

H. An advanced system configuration tool with diagnostics features.

I. A critical step in managing multi-boot setups effectively.

J. An interface offering AI-powered performance optimization.

Test V: Essay Question

Instructions: Write a concise and well-organized essay on the following topic. Provide specific examples to support your answer.

Question:

How do advanced BIOS/UEFI configurations, multi-boot systems, and cloud-connected PCs contribute to enhancing productivity and collaboration in modern digital work environments?

Chapter 5

System Maintenance in the AI Era

Chapter 5 explores the transformative impact of artificial intelligence and machine learning on system maintenance in the modern era. From AI-powered cleanup tools that optimize storage and performance to predictive maintenance techniques that preemptively address hardware issues, this chapter highlights the tools and technologies redefining PC upkeep. It also examines the role of performance monitoring tools integrated with AI for dynamic optimizations. Through practical examples and actionable insights, this chapter provides a roadmap for leveraging AI to ensure systems operate efficiently and reliably in an increasingly demanding digital landscape.

Automated System Cleanup Tools with AI

AI-powered cleanup tools automate the removal of unnecessary files, optimizing storage and performance. These tools analyze user behavior to identify redundant data and suggest customized cleanup strategies.

Real-World Example:

CCleaner's AI-enhanced version scans for unused applications and large redundant files, helping users free up valuable disk space effortlessly.

Predictive Maintenance with Machine Learning

Machine learning algorithms in predictive maintenance monitor system health, detecting potential failures before they occur. They analyze hardware telemetry and usage patterns to provide actionable insights.

Real-World Example:

Lenovo's Vantage software uses predictive analytics to alert users about impending battery degradation, allowing proactive replacements.

Tools for Optimizing and Monitoring System Performance

Modern tools like HWMonitor, GPU-Z, and Task Manager provide detailed insights into system performance. AI integration enables automated optimizations, such as adjusting fan speeds and reallocating resources.

Real-World Example:

Gamers using MSI Afterburner can dynamically adjust GPU settings based on real-time performance metrics, ensuring smooth gameplay.

Conclusion

AI and machine learning are transforming system maintenance, offering predictive tools and automated solutions that enhance reliability and performance. These technologies ensure that PCs operate efficiently, extending their lifespan and usability.

Comprehensive Test Assessment for Chapter 5

Test I: Multiple-Choice Questions

Instructions: Read each question carefully. Select the correct answer by encircling the letter of your choice.

1. What is the primary function of AI-powered cleanup tools?

   A. Installing new software

   B. Automating file removal and optimizing storage

   C. Predicting hardware failures

   D. Enhancing system boot speed

2. Which AI-enhanced tool scans for unused applications and large redundant files?

   A. Lenovo Vantage

   B. MSI Afterburner

   C. CCleaner

   D. Task Manager

3. What is the purpose of predictive maintenance with machine learning?

   A. To remove unnecessary files

   B. To monitor system health and detect potential failures

   C. To automate system updates

   D. To increase storage capacity

4. Which software alerts users about potential hardware issues like battery degradation?

   A. GPU-Z

   B. HWMonitor

C. Lenovo Vantage

D. MSI Afterburner

5. What does MSI Afterburner allow gamers to do?

   A. Optimize file storage

   B. Adjust GPU settings dynamically based on performance metrics

   C. Monitor hardware telemetry

   D. Automate malware detection

6. How do tools like HWMonitor and GPU-Z support system maintenance?

   A. By providing detailed performance insights

   B. By automating file organization

   C. By predicting software compatibility issues

   D. By creating virtual machine environments

7. What is a key benefit of AI in system maintenance?

   A. Manual performance optimization

   B. Preemptive hardware failure detection

   C. Increased storage without upgrades

   D. Reduced need for cybersecurity measures

8. Which of the following is an example of dynamic optimization in system maintenance?

   A. Automated disk defragmentation

   B. AI-driven fan speed adjustments during high performance

   C. Pre-installed monitoring software

   D. Static hardware configurations

9. What feature of AI-powered maintenance tools enhances efficiency in demanding environments?

   A. Predictive analytics and automation

B. Manual file classification

C. Preemptive software updates

D. Advanced network integration

10. What is the overarching goal of AI and machine learning in system maintenance?

A. To eliminate the need for IT professionals

B. To ensure efficient and reliable PC operations

C. To reduce the lifespan of hardware components

D. To replace all manual maintenance tools

Test II: Identification

Instructions: Identify the term or concept being described. Write your answer in the space provided.

1. A tool that uses AI to scan for unused applications and optimize storage.

2. The process of detecting hardware issues before they occur using machine learning.

3. Software that alerts users about potential battery degradation.

4. A performance optimization tool used by gamers to adjust GPU settings dynamically.

5. A system monitoring tool that provides insights into hardware performance metrics.

6. An AI-driven technique for reallocating resources to maintain system performance.

7. The type of telemetry data used to predict system health and failures.

8. A tool for dynamically optimizing fan speeds and GPU performance.

9. The role of machine learning in identifying usage patterns for maintenance.

10. The software feature enabling proactive system cleanup strategies.

Test III: True-or-False Questions

Instructions: Read each statement carefully. Write T if the statement is true and F if it is false.

1. Predictive maintenance relies on machine learning to forecast potential system failures.
2. AI cleanup tools require manual intervention to remove unnecessary files.
3. CCleaner is an example of a predictive maintenance tool.
4. Lenovo Vantage alerts users about potential hardware failures, such as battery issues.
5. HWMonitor and GPU-Z are used for real-time malware detection.
6. Dynamic optimization involves automating resource allocation based on performance needs.
7. AI-powered tools can extend the lifespan of PCs by enhancing reliability.
8. MSI Afterburner is used to manage cloud storage solutions.
9. Predictive analytics in maintenance eliminates the need for user decision-making.
10. AI tools in maintenance help reduce manual workload while improving efficiency.

Test IV: Matching-Type Questions

Instructions: Match the items in Column A with their corresponding descriptions in Column B. Write the letter of the correct match on the blank provided.

Column A

1. CCleaner
2. Lenovo Vantage
3. MSI Afterburner
4. HWMonitor
5. Predictive Maintenance
6. Dynamic Optimization
7. Machine Learning
8. GPU-Z
9. Fan Speed Adjustment
10. AI Cleanup Tools

Column B

A. Detects battery degradation and alerts users proactively.

B. Monitors system performance, providing insights into hardware metrics.

C. Adjusts GPU performance dynamically during gameplay.

D. Removes unnecessary files and optimizes storage.

E. Forecasts potential hardware issues using telemetry data.

F. Automates resource allocation to enhance system performance.

G. Analyzes usage patterns to suggest maintenance strategies.

H. A tool for optimizing graphics card performance metrics.

I. AI-driven feature for managing system cooling based on

performance.

J. Streamlines storage by analyzing redundant data and files.

Test V: Essay Question

Instructions: Write a concise and well-organized essay on the following topic. Provide specific examples to support your answer.

Question:
Discuss how artificial intelligence and machine learning are revolutionizing system maintenance. Highlight the benefits of AI-powered cleanup tools, predictive maintenance, and performance optimization using real-world examples.

Chapter 6

Advanced Networking for a Connected Future

Chapter 6 delves into the cutting-edge advancements in networking that are shaping a more connected future. It highlights the game-changing capabilities of Wi-Fi 7, with its unprecedented speeds and multi-link operation ensuring seamless performance for even the most device-intensive environments. This chapter also explores the challenges of troubleshooting IoT devices in modern home networks and the pivotal role of blockchain technology in enhancing network security. Through real-world examples and practical insights, this chapter equips readers with the knowledge to navigate and optimize the increasingly interconnected digital landscape of 2025.

Wi-Fi 7 and Beyond: Features and Benefits

Wi-Fi 7 introduces unprecedented speeds, low latency, and improved device capacity. Its multi-link operation (MLO) ensures stable connections, even in congested environments.

Real-World Example:

A smart home with over 50 connected devices operates seamlessly on a Wi-Fi 7 router, providing uninterrupted streaming, gaming, and IoT functionality.

Troubleshooting IoT Devices in a Home Network

IoT device troubleshooting involves ensuring compatibility, securing connections, and diagnosing network issues. Tools like Fing and Wireshark aid in identifying and resolving connectivity problems.

Real-World Example:

A homeowner resolves intermittent smart thermostat connectivity by using Fing to pinpoint signal interference from a nearby router.

Role of Blockchain in Secure Networking

Blockchain technology enhances network security by enabling decentralized authentication and data integrity verification. Its applications include secure IoT ecosystems and encrypted communications.

Real-World Example:

Helium Network uses blockchain to create a decentralized wireless network, ensuring secure data transmission for IoT devices.

Conclusion

Advanced networking technologies in 2025 address the growing demand for speed, security, and reliability. From Wi-Fi 7 to blockchain-enabled networks, these innovations ensure seamless connectivity and robust protection in an increasingly interconnected world.

Comprehensive Test Assessment for Chapter 6

Test I: Multiple-Choice Questions

Instructions: Read each question carefully. Select the correct answer by encircling the letter of your choice.

1. What is a key feature of Wi-Fi 7 that enhances connectivity?

   A. Single-link operation

   B. Multi-link operation (MLO)

   C. Blockchain integration

   D. Virtual machine support

2. How does Wi-Fi 7 ensure stable connections in congested environments?

   A. By reducing device capacity

   B. By implementing multi-link operation (MLO)

   C. By disabling low-latency functions

   D. By encrypting data packets

3. What is the primary purpose of tools like Fing and Wireshark in IoT networks?

   A. Installing IoT devices

   B. Diagnosing and resolving connectivity issues

   C. Enhancing blockchain security

   D. Improving device capacity

4. What network security benefit does blockchain provide?

   A. High-speed data transfer

   B. Decentralized authentication and data integrity verification

C. Reduced latency in smart homes

D. Compatibility with all IoT devices

5. What example demonstrates the application of blockchain in networking?

   A. Wi-Fi 7 routers with multi-link operation

   B. Helium Network creating decentralized wireless networks

   C. Smart thermostat troubleshooting with Fing

   D. Wireshark detecting hardware failures

6. What is the benefit of Wi-Fi 7 for smart homes?

   A. Improved system cooling

   B. Seamless operation for multiple connected devices

   C. Automated hardware diagnostics

   D. Reduced data encryption requirements

7. Which technology enhances IoT ecosystem security?

   A. Machine learning algorithms

   B. Decentralized blockchain technology

   C. High-speed SSDs

   D. AI-driven overclocking

8. How does Fing assist with IoT troubleshooting?

   A. By providing encryption for network connections

   B. By pinpointing signal interference and connectivity issues

   C. By upgrading device firmware

   D. By managing network bandwidth

9. What does blockchain ensure in secure networking?

   A. Higher device capacity

   B. Encrypted communications and decentralized verification

   C. Faster wireless speeds

   D. Improved file sharing across devices

10. What does multi-link operation (MLO) in Wi-Fi 7 enable?

    A. Single-device connectivity

    B. Stable and uninterrupted connections in busy networks

    C. Blockchain integration for IoT devices

    D. Real-time system performance monitoring

Test II: Identification

Instructions: Identify the term or concept being described. Write your answer in the space provided.

1. The Wi-Fi technology that offers low latency and supports multiple connected devices in congested environments.

2. The process of diagnosing connectivity issues in IoT networks.

3. A tool used to pinpoint signal interference and resolve IoT connectivity problems.

4. A technology that enhances network security through decentralized authentication.

5. An example of a decentralized wireless network powered by blockchain.

6. The feature of Wi-Fi 7 that ensures stable connections across multiple devices.

7. The type of devices that benefit most from Wi-Fi 7's high-speed connections.

8. A network security application that prevents unauthorized data access in IoT systems.

9. A tool for monitoring and troubleshooting network traffic in home networks.

10. The primary benefit of blockchain technology in networking environments.

Test III: True-or-False Questions

Instructions: Read each statement carefully. Write T if the statement is true and F if it is false.

1. Wi-Fi 7's multi-link operation ensures seamless connectivity for multiple devices.
2. Blockchain technology is not applicable to IoT ecosystem security.
3. Fing and Wireshark are tools used to diagnose connectivity issues in IoT networks.
4. Wi-Fi 7 introduces higher latency compared to previous wireless technologies.
5. Helium Network demonstrates blockchain's application in decentralized wireless networks.
6. IoT device troubleshooting involves ensuring compatibility and diagnosing network issues.
7. Blockchain enhances network security by centralizing authentication processes.
8. Multi-link operation in Wi-Fi 7 ensures stable connections even in busy environments.
9. Wi-Fi 7 is ideal for use in smart homes with many connected devices.
10. Troubleshooting tools like Fing help detect and fix signal interference in IoT setups.

Test IV: Matching-Type Questions

Instructions: Match the items in Column A with their corresponding descriptions in Column B. Write the letter of the correct match on the blank provided.

Column A

1. Wi-Fi 7
2. Blockchain
3. Fing
4. Helium Network
5. Multi-Link Operation (MLO)
6. IoT Troubleshooting
7. Wireshark
8. Decentralized Authentication
9. Smart Home Devices
10. Encrypted Communications

Column B

A. A technology that ensures stable and seamless connections in Wi-Fi 7.

B. A wireless network powered by blockchain for secure data transmission.

C. Enables secure IoT ecosystems by verifying data integrity.

D. Used to identify and resolve connectivity problems in IoT devices.

E. Ideal for managing multiple connected devices in smart homes.

F. Enhances network security by decentralizing verification processes.

G. Introduces unprecedented speeds and low latency for wireless networking.

H. Assists in diagnosing network traffic and troubleshooting issues.

I. Protects sensitive information in IoT networks.

J. A tool used for detecting signal interference in home networks.

Test V: Essay Question

Instructions: Write a concise and well-organized essay on the following topic. Provide specific examples to support your answer.

Question:
How are Wi-Fi 7, IoT troubleshooting tools, and blockchain technology shaping the future of networking in 2025? Discuss their roles in ensuring connectivity, reliability, and security.

Chapter 7

Cybersecurity Challenges in 2025

Chapter 7 examines the evolving cybersecurity landscape of 2025, highlighting the challenges posed by sophisticated ransomware attacks and the measures needed to counter them. It explores the growing importance of zero-trust architecture in safeguarding small businesses and the implementation of advanced encryption standards to protect sensitive communications. Through detailed discussions and real-world examples, this chapter provides insights into proactive strategies and technologies that ensure robust defense against an increasingly complex and dynamic array of cybersecurity threats.

Trends in Ransomware and Countermeasures

Ransomware attacks have grown more sophisticated, targeting both individuals and organizations. Modern ransomware uses encryption techniques that render files inaccessible until a ransom is paid. Countermeasures include regular backups, robust endpoint protection, and zero-trust security frameworks.

Real-World Example:

In 2025, a major healthcare provider thwarted a ransomware attack by employing immutable backups and AI-driven threat detection, ensuring patient data remained secure.

Role of Zero-Trust Architecture in Small Businesses

Zero-trust architecture assumes no user or device is inherently trustworthy. It employs multi-factor authentication (MFA), micro-segmentation, and continuous monitoring to protect sensitive data.

Real-World Example:

A small e-commerce business implemented a zero-trust model, significantly reducing unauthorized access and enhancing data security across its payment systems.

Advanced Encryption Standards for Secure Communications

Encryption standards like AES-256 and quantum-resistant algorithms safeguard communications against evolving threats. These standards are critical for secure messaging, financial transactions, and government communications.

Real-World Example:

A financial institution adopted post-quantum cryptography protocols to future-proof its transaction systems against quantum computing threats.

Conclusion

Cybersecurity in 2025 requires proactive strategies to combat evolving threats. From ransomware defense to zero-trust implementations and advanced encryption, these measures ensure robust protection for digital assets in an increasingly complex threat landscape.

Comprehensive Test Assessment for Chapter 7

Test I: Multiple-Choice Questions

Instructions: Read each question carefully. Select the correct answer by encircling the letter of your choice.

1. What is a key characteristic of modern ransomware attacks?

    A. Lack of encryption techniques

    B. Use of encryption to make files inaccessible

    C. Targeting only small businesses

    D. Inability to affect financial systems

2. Which of the following is an effective countermeasure against ransomware?

    A. Disabling endpoint protection

    B. Relying solely on user vigilance

    C. Implementing immutable backups and AI-driven threat detection

    D. Avoiding multi-factor authentication

3. What does zero-trust architecture assume about users and devices?

    A. They are inherently trustworthy

    B. They must verify their identity before access is granted

    C. They are not required to use MFA

    D. They are protected by default

4. What cybersecurity framework uses MFA, micro-segmentation, and continuous monitoring?

    A. Blockchain authentication

B. Zero-trust architecture

C. AI-driven endpoint protection

D. Post-quantum cryptography

5. Which encryption standard is designed to protect against future quantum computing threats?

   A. DES-128

   B. SHA-512

   C. AES-256 and quantum-resistant algorithms

   D. Legacy encryption protocols

6. How did a major healthcare provider prevent a ransomware attack in 2025?

   A. By paying the ransom quickly

   B. By using immutable backups and AI-driven detection

   C. By avoiding endpoint protection

   D. By disabling multi-factor authentication

7. What is the role of advanced encryption standards in cybersecurity?

   A. To increase ransomware susceptibility

   B. To safeguard communications and financial transactions

   C. To eliminate the need for backups

   D. To simplify cybersecurity protocols

8. What is an example of a real-world application of post-quantum cryptography?

   A. Protecting CAD files in cloud storage

   B. Future-proofing financial transaction systems against quantum threats

   C. Enhancing device connectivity in IoT ecosystems

   D. Automating GPU performance adjustments

9. What is a key advantage of zero-trust architecture for small businesses?

    A. Reducing the need for encryption protocols

    B. Enhancing data security by minimizing unauthorized access

    C. Allowing unrestricted device access

    D. Avoiding the use of multi-factor authentication

10. Which technology ensures data security through decentralized authentication and integrity verification?

    A. Ransomware encryption

    B. Endpoint protection tools

    C. Blockchain

    D. AES-128 encryption

Test II: Identification

Instructions: Identify the term or concept being described. Write your answer in the space provided.

1. A cybersecurity framework that assumes no user or device is inherently trustworthy.

2. The process of safeguarding financial systems against quantum computing threats.

3. A key component of zero-trust architecture that requires users to verify their identity.

4. An encryption standard designed for secure communications and financial transactions.

5. A tool that helps protect sensitive data by employing continuous monitoring and segmentation.

6. The method used by ransomware to make files inaccessible until a ransom is paid.

7. A proactive strategy used by a healthcare provider to thwart a ransomware attack in 2025.

8. The role of AI-driven tools in detecting and preventing cybersecurity threats.

9. A cybersecurity threat that specifically targets individuals and organizations by encrypting data.

10. A real-world example of a business adopting a zero-trust model to enhance payment security.

Test III: True-or-False Questions

Instructions: Read each statement carefully. Write T if the statement is true and F if it is false.

1. Zero-trust architecture assumes all devices are trustworthy by default.

2. Immutable backups are an effective defense against ransomware attacks.

3. Advanced encryption standards like AES-256 protect against quantum computing threats.

4. A small e-commerce business can enhance data security with zero-trust architecture.

5. Post-quantum cryptography is irrelevant to financial transaction systems.

6. AI-driven threat detection reduces the risk of ransomware attacks.

7. Ransomware attacks in 2025 do not use encryption techniques.

8. Zero-trust models eliminate the need for continuous monitoring.

9. Multi-factor authentication (MFA) is a key feature of zero-trust architecture.

10. Advanced encryption standards are critical for protecting sensitive communications.

Test IV: Matching-Type Questions

Instructions: Match the items in Column A with their corresponding descriptions in Column B. Write the letter of the correct match on the blank provided.

Column A

1. Ransomware
2. Zero-Trust Architecture
3. Immutable Backups
4. AES-256 Encryption
5. AI-Driven Threat Detection
6. Multi-Factor Authentication (MFA)
7. Post-Quantum Cryptography
8. Micro-Segmentation
9. Continuous Monitoring
10. Healthcare Cybersecurity

Column B

A. Divides a network into smaller parts to minimize unauthorized access.

B. A framework that assumes no user or device is inherently trustworthy.

C. Ensures secure communications and transactions against evolving threats.

D. A cybersecurity measure that safeguards data by using multiple authentication steps.

E. Future-proof encryption protecting against quantum computing threats.

F. A type of malware that encrypts files, demanding payment for access.

G. An AI-based tool used to detect and mitigate cybersecurity threats.

H. Protects sensitive data by creating unchangeable backup copies.

I. Uses AI and backups to thwart a ransomware attack.

J. Monitors systems continuously to detect potential threats.

Test V: Essay Question

Instructions: Write a concise and well-organized essay on the following topic. Provide specific examples to support your answer.

Question:

Discuss how ransomware, zero-trust architecture, and advanced encryption standards are addressing cybersecurity challenges in 2025. Include real-world examples to illustrate their impact.

Chapter 8

Leveraging Virtualization and Cloud Computing

Chapter 8 delves into the transformative impact of virtualization and cloud computing on modern IT operations. It explores how cloud-based troubleshooting enhances efficiency, how virtualization enables testing and training in controlled environments, and the innovative role of virtualization in gaming. Through real-world examples and practical insights, this chapter highlights the versatility of these technologies and their potential to revolutionize diverse fields, from IT management to entertainment.

Benefits of Cloud-Based Troubleshooting

Cloud-based troubleshooting tools offer remote access, automated diagnostics, and real-time monitoring. They enable IT teams to address issues efficiently, regardless of location.

Real-World Example:

A global IT firm resolved a critical server outage using Microsoft Azure's cloud troubleshooting tools, restoring operations within minutes.

Using Virtualization for Testing and Training

Virtualization allows users to create isolated environments for software testing and employee training. Tools like VMware and VirtualBox simulate diverse operating systems and network configurations.

Real-World Example:

A university employed virtualization to provide students with hands-on experience in cybersecurity labs, simulating real-world attack scenarios.

Gaming in Virtual Environments: A New Frontier

Virtualization is transforming gaming by enabling cloud-based game hosting and testing. Players can enjoy high-quality gaming experiences without requiring powerful local hardware.

Real-World Example:

NVIDIA's GeForce Now platform leverages virtualization to deliver AAA gaming experiences on low-spec devices via cloud streaming.

Conclusion

Virtualization and cloud computing are revolutionizing IT operations, offering scalable, efficient, and secure solutions. From troubleshooting and testing to gaming, these technologies are paving the way for innovative applications in diverse fields.

Comprehensive Test Assessment for Chapter 8

Test I: Multiple-Choice Questions

Instructions: Read each question carefully. Select the correct answer by encircling the letter of your choice.

1. What is a key benefit of cloud-based troubleshooting tools?

   A. Eliminating hardware compatibility issues

   B. Providing remote access and automated diagnostics

   C. Enhancing GPU performance for gaming

   D. Simulating network configurations

2. Which platform helped a global IT firm resolve a critical server outage?

   A. VMware

   B. Microsoft Azure

   C. NVIDIA GeForce Now

   D. VirtualBox

3. How does virtualization support testing and training?

   A. By offering pre-installed operating systems

   B. By creating isolated environments for simulations

   C. By automating diagnostic processes

   D. By optimizing cloud storage

4. What tool is commonly used to simulate diverse operating systems and network configurations?

   A. NVIDIA RTX 5000

   B. Microsoft OneDrive

C. VMware or VirtualBox

D. Fing

5. What does NVIDIA's GeForce Now platform offer to gamers?

    A. Cloud-based hosting and high-quality gaming on low-spec devices

    B. Enhanced AR support for gaming applications

    C. Integrated troubleshooting for server outages

    D. Virtual machine management for IT professionals

6. Which field benefits most from virtualization in hands-on training?

    A. Entertainment and media

    B. Cybersecurity labs and real-world simulations

    C. Graphic design and 3D modeling

    D. Financial analytics

7. What is a primary advantage of virtualization in gaming?

    A. Eliminating the need for powerful local hardware

    B. Reducing latency in cloud troubleshooting

    C. Automating diagnostic software

    D. Securing data through encryption

8. How do cloud-based troubleshooting tools enhance IT operations?

    A. By requiring physical access to systems

    B. By automating updates and manual fixes

    C. By providing real-time monitoring and remote access

    D. By managing multi-boot system setups

9. What does virtualization enable for software testing?

    A. Real-time error correction

B. Cross-platform compatibility

C. Isolated environments to simulate diverse scenarios

D. GPU optimization for resource-heavy applications

10. Which technology is revolutionizing IT operations by offering scalable and secure solutions?

A. AI-powered diagnostics

B. Virtualization and cloud computing

C. Blockchain-enabled systems

D. AR/VR gaming environments

Test II: Identification

Instructions: Identify the term or concept being described. Write your answer in the space provided.

1. A cloud-based platform used to resolve critical server outages efficiently.

2. A virtualization tool commonly employed for testing and training in IT.

3. A platform that provides cloud-based gaming experiences on low-spec devices.

4. The process of creating isolated environments for software simulations.

5. A benefit of cloud-based troubleshooting tools that enables addressing issues remotely.

6. The technology transforming gaming by hosting games on the cloud.

7. A field where universities use virtualization for hands-on training.

8. A tool that allows simulations of diverse network configurations.

9. The technology enabling scalable, efficient, and secure IT solutions.

10. A real-world application of virtualization in gaming for hosting AAA titles.

Test III: True-or-False Questions

Instructions: Read each statement carefully. Write T if the statement is true and F if it is false.

1. Cloud-based troubleshooting tools require IT teams to be physically present at the site of the issue.
2. Virtualization supports testing by creating isolated environments for diverse scenarios.
3. Microsoft Azure is a cloud platform used for gaming virtualization.
4. NVIDIA's GeForce Now platform eliminates the need for powerful gaming hardware.
5. Virtualization is used in cybersecurity labs to simulate real-world attack scenarios.
6. Cloud-based troubleshooting tools offer real-time monitoring capabilities.
7. VirtualBox is a tool commonly used for network optimization.
8. Gaming virtualization requires high-end local hardware to function properly.
9. Cloud computing enhances IT operations by providing scalable and secure solutions.
10. Virtualization in gaming allows players to enjoy AAA titles on low-spec devices via cloud streaming.

Test IV: Matching-Type Questions

Instructions: Match the items in Column A with their corresponding descriptions in Column B. Write the letter of the correct match on the blank provided.

Column A

1. Microsoft Azure
2. VMware
3. NVIDIA GeForce Now
4. VirtualBox
5. Cloud-Based Troubleshooting
6. Isolated Environments
7. Cybersecurity Labs
8. Cloud Gaming
9. Real-Time Monitoring
10. Scalable IT Solutions

Column B

A. Creates simulations for diverse operating systems and networks.

B. A cloud platform used to resolve server outages efficiently.

C. Supports AAA gaming experiences on low-spec devices.

D. Enables addressing IT issues remotely and efficiently.

E. Used to simulate real-world attack scenarios for training purposes.

F. Allows testing and training in controlled and secure settings.

G. Provides automated diagnostics and resource monitoring.

H. Enables hosting of games without reliance on local hardware.

I. A virtualization tool commonly used for IT operations.

J. A primary benefit of virtualization and cloud computing for IT management.

Test V: Essay Question

Instructions: Write a concise and well-organized essay on the following topic. Provide specific examples to support your answer.

Question:
Discuss how virtualization and cloud computing are transforming IT operations, testing, and gaming in 2025. Provide real-world examples to illustrate their impact on efficiency, scalability, and innovation.

Chapter 9

Advanced Troubleshooting Techniques

Chapter 9 focuses on advanced troubleshooting techniques essential for navigating the complexities of modern technology ecosystems. It examines the use of AI-driven diagnostic tools to enhance efficiency, the unique challenges of resolving hardware issues in VR/AR devices, and practical strategies for addressing cross-platform conflicts. By highlighting real-world examples and actionable approaches, this chapter equips readers with the skills and insights needed to tackle sophisticated troubleshooting scenarios in an increasingly interconnected digital world.

Using AI-Driven Diagnostic Tools

AI diagnostic tools analyze large datasets to detect anomalies and suggest tailored solutions. They enhance efficiency and accuracy in identifying complex system issues.

Real-World Example:

IBM Watson AIOps proactively identified and resolved a memory leak in a critical application, preventing system downtime for a multinational corporation.

Troubleshooting Hardware Issues in VR/AR Devices

Diagnosing VR/AR hardware involves testing sensors, calibrating displays, and ensuring firmware compatibility. Specialized tools and software are essential for identifying and resolving issues.

Real-World Example:

A VR arcade used HTC's diagnostic suite to troubleshoot motion tracking problems, ensuring a seamless customer experience.

Practical Approaches to Resolve Cross-Platform Conflicts

Cross-platform conflicts arise in environments running multiple operating systems or software versions. Solutions include using compatibility layers, virtualization, and middleware tools.

Real-World Example:

A gaming studio resolved engine compatibility issues between Windows and Linux builds by implementing Proton, a compatibility tool developed by Valve.

Conclusion

Advanced troubleshooting techniques are critical in an era of diverse and rapidly evolving technology ecosystems. By leveraging AI diagnostic tools, addressing hardware challenges in VR/AR, and resolving cross-platform conflicts, IT professionals and end-users alike can maintain optimal system functionality. As technology becomes more integrated into everyday life, these advanced methods will continue to evolve, ensuring systems remain reliable and effective.

Comprehensive Test Assessment for Chapter 9

Test I: Multiple-Choice Questions

Instructions: Read each question carefully. Select the correct answer by encircling the letter of your choice.

1. What is the primary function of AI-driven diagnostic tools?
   A. To replace hardware components
   B. To detect anomalies and provide tailored solutions
   C. To optimize gaming performance
   D. To troubleshoot display calibration issues

2. How did IBM Watson AIOps assist a multinational corporation?
   A. By preventing unauthorized access
   B. By resolving a memory leak in a critical application
   C. By optimizing hardware for VR gaming
   D. By managing cloud storage

3. What is a key challenge in troubleshooting VR/AR hardware?
   A. Ensuring network compatibility
   B. Testing sensors and calibrating displays
   C. Enhancing GPU performance
   D. Automating system updates

4. Which tool was used by a VR arcade to troubleshoot motion tracking problems?
   A. VirtualBox
   B. Proton

C. HTC's diagnostic suite

D. VMware

5. What causes cross-platform conflicts in modern environments?

   A. Outdated hardware components

   B. Running multiple operating systems or software versions

   C. Incompatible network configurations

   D. Lack of AI-driven tools

6. What solution did a gaming studio use to address cross-platform compatibility issues?

   A. Cloud-based troubleshooting

   B. Proton, a compatibility tool developed by Valve

   C. VR motion tracking software

   D. Multi-factor authentication

7. Which technology is most effective for resolving engine compatibility issues between operating systems?

   A. Machine learning algorithms

   B. Compatibility layers and middleware tools

   C. Blockchain authentication

   D. Real-time ray tracing

8. Why are AI diagnostic tools crucial in modern troubleshooting?

   A. They eliminate the need for user input

   B. They analyze large datasets to enhance efficiency and accuracy

   C. They focus solely on hardware optimizations

   D. They are exclusively designed for gaming applications

9. What is a common issue in VR/AR troubleshooting?

    A. Managing cloud resources

    B. Ensuring firmware compatibility

    C. Detecting unauthorized system access

    D. Resolving memory leaks

10. What is the primary goal of advanced troubleshooting techniques?

    A. To enhance visual performance in games

    B. To ensure systems remain reliable and effective

    C. To eliminate manual diagnostics entirely

    D. To improve cross-platform network speeds

Test II: Identification

Instructions: Identify the term or concept being described. Write your answer in the space provided.

1. A diagnostic tool that analyzes large datasets to detect anomalies and suggest solutions.

2. The process of troubleshooting VR/AR hardware by testing sensors and calibrating displays.

3. A tool used by a VR arcade to resolve motion tracking issues.

4. The compatibility tool developed by Valve for resolving engine conflicts between operating systems.

5. The primary function of AI-driven tools in system diagnostics.

6. A real-world example of AI resolving a critical application issue in a multinational corporation.

7. A common cause of cross-platform conflicts in modern environments.

8. The type of tools used to ensure firmware compatibility in VR/AR devices.

9. A solution used for managing conflicts in environments running multiple OS versions.

10. The primary goal of advanced troubleshooting in diverse technology ecosystems.

Test III: True-or-False Questions

Instructions: Read each statement carefully. Write T if the statement is true and F if it is false.

1. AI-driven diagnostic tools can resolve system issues without user intervention.
2. Cross-platform conflicts arise only in single-operating system environments.
3. Proton is a middleware tool used to address software compatibility issues.
4. Troubleshooting VR/AR hardware involves testing sensors and ensuring firmware compatibility.
5. AI diagnostic tools are designed specifically for gaming applications.
6. HTC's diagnostic suite is used for resolving motion tracking problems in VR devices.
7. Compatibility layers can help resolve conflicts between different software environments.
8. AI tools are ineffective in detecting memory leaks in critical applications.
9. Advanced troubleshooting techniques improve the reliability of interconnected systems.
10. Resolving cross-platform conflicts is unnecessary in modern technology ecosystems.

Test IV: Matching-Type Questions

Instructions: Match the items in Column A with their corresponding descriptions in Column B. Write the letter of the correct match on the blank provided.

Column A

1. AI Diagnostic Tools
2. IBM Watson AIOps
3. HTC Diagnostic Suite
4. Proton
5. Firmware Compatibility
6. Cross-Platform Conflicts
7. Middleware Tools
8. VR/AR Troubleshooting
9. Anomaly Detection
10. Advanced Troubleshooting

Column B

A. Used by a VR arcade to resolve motion tracking problems.

B. Addresses issues caused by multiple operating systems or software versions.

C. A tool for ensuring engine compatibility between Windows and Linux builds.

D. The process of testing sensors and calibrating displays in modern devices.

E. Identifies and resolves memory leaks in critical applications.

F. Enhances efficiency by analyzing large datasets to detect issues.

G. Ensures software and hardware compatibility in devices like VR headsets.

H. Improves system reliability in interconnected ecosystems.

I. Tools that bridge compatibility gaps between software platforms.

J. The detection of irregularities in system performance or data.

Test V: Essay Question

Instructions: Write a concise and well-organized essay on the following topic. Provide specific examples to support your answer.

Question:

Discuss the role of AI-driven diagnostic tools, VR/AR troubleshooting, and cross-platform conflict resolution in ensuring system reliability and efficiency in modern technology ecosystems. Use real-world examples to illustrate your points.

Chapter 10

The Future of PC Troubleshooting

Chapter 10 explores the exciting future of PC troubleshooting, focusing on emerging trends and technologies poised to transform the field. It examines advancements such as self-healing systems, quantum computing diagnostics, and collaborative AI platforms, highlighting their potential to revolutionize how issues are identified and resolved. Additionally, this chapter provides predictions for troubleshooting in 2030 and offers actionable insights on preparing for the dominance of quantum computing and AI. Through real-world examples and forward-looking analysis, it emphasizes the importance of adaptation and innovation in navigating the rapidly evolving tech landscape.

Emerging Trends in Troubleshooting Technology

The future of PC troubleshooting will be shaped by several key technological trends:

Self-Healing Systems: PCs capable of diagnosing and repairing themselves autonomously using embedded AI.

Quantum Computing Diagnostics: Tools designed to troubleshoot quantum-based systems as they become more prevalent.

Collaborative AI Platforms: Systems where multiple AI tools collaborate to resolve complex issues more efficiently.

Real-World Example:

Dell Technologies is developing self-healing firmware that can recover from corruption without user intervention, providing a glimpse into autonomous system troubleshooting.

Predictions for PC Troubleshooting in 2030

By 2030, troubleshooting will likely be:

1. Fully integrated into cloud ecosystems, enabling seamless remote diagnostics.
2. Guided by virtual reality (VR) interfaces that allow technicians to interact with 3D models of hardware.
3. Supported by quantum-enhanced AI tools for unmatched diagnostic precision.

Real-World Example:

Google's advances in AI suggest that future troubleshooting may involve conversational AI interfaces capable of resolving issues through natural language exchanges.

Preparing for the Era of Quantum and AI Dominance

As quantum computing and AI dominate the technological landscape, preparing for these advancements is essential:

Training Programs: IT professionals must acquire skills in quantum mechanics and AI-driven tools.

Adapting Infrastructure: Organizations should transition to systems capable of supporting quantum and AI-based troubleshooting.

Research and Collaboration: Continuous research into emerging technologies and collaboration with tech leaders will ensure readiness.

Real-World Example:

IBM has launched educational programs to train engineers in quantum computing basics, addressing the growing demand for skilled professionals in this domain.

Conclusion

The future of PC troubleshooting is an exciting blend of innovation and necessity. As self-healing systems, quantum diagnostics, and collaborative AI platforms redefine the field, users and IT professionals must adapt to stay ahead. With technology progressing at an unprecedented pace, the tools and techniques of tomorrow promise to make troubleshooting faster, more accurate, and more accessible than ever before.

Comprehensive Test Assessment for Chapter 10

Test I: Multiple-Choice Questions

Instructions: Read each question carefully. Select the correct answer by encircling the letter of your choice.

1. What is a key feature of self-healing systems in future PC troubleshooting?

    A. They require manual repairs from technicians

    B. They autonomously diagnose and repair issues using embedded AI

    C. They prevent all hardware issues from occurring

    D. They only function with cloud-based services

2. Which technology is expected to help troubleshoot quantum-based systems?

    A. Cloud diagnostics

    B. Virtual reality interfaces

    C. Quantum computing diagnostics

    D. AI-powered task managers

3. What role do collaborative AI platforms play in the future of troubleshooting?

    A. They replace human technicians entirely

    B. They allow multiple AI tools to collaborate for more efficient problem resolution

    C. They manage user hardware interfaces

    D. They limit troubleshooting to software-related issues

4. How will troubleshooting likely be guided by 2030?

   A. By command-line interfaces

   B. By virtual reality interfaces for interacting with 3D models of hardware

   C. By manual diagnostic tools

   D. By decentralized cloud-based systems

5. What is a predicted outcome for PC troubleshooting in 2030?

   A. Reduced use of cloud technologies

   B. No reliance on AI tools

   C. Full integration into cloud ecosystems for remote diagnostics

   D. Manual tools for diagnostics

6. What is an example of self-healing technology being developed by Dell Technologies?

   A. AI-powered hard drive repair tools

   B. Firmware that can recover from corruption without user intervention

   C. Cloud-based backup services

   D. Real-time system monitoring software

7. What is a significant feature of quantum-enhanced AI tools?

   A. Slower processing speeds

   B. Unmatched diagnostic precision for future troubleshooting

   C. Limited application in troubleshooting

   D. Reduced power consumption

8. What does the future of troubleshooting in 2030 involve?

   A. Relying exclusively on AI

B. Cloud-based systems for remote diagnostics and quantum computing diagnostics

C. Discontinuation of AI tools

D. Manual troubleshooting methods

9. What training is essential for IT professionals in the future?

A. Basic hardware repair skills

B. Quantum mechanics and AI-driven tools

C. General software knowledge

D. Networking protocols

10. What is IBM's initiative to prepare professionals for quantum computing and AI dominance?

A. Launching educational programs on basic quantum computing concepts

B. Replacing AI tools with manual systems

C. Eliminating the need for training programs

D. Limiting AI in troubleshooting

Test II: Identification

Instructions: Identify the term or concept being described. Write your answer in the space provided.

1. A system that autonomously diagnoses and repairs itself using embedded AI.

2. A future technology tool designed to troubleshoot quantum-based systems.

3. The process of having multiple AI tools collaborate to resolve issues more efficiently.

4. A 2030 prediction for troubleshooting, involving the use of virtual reality interfaces.

5. The field of study required to prepare IT professionals for the era of quantum computing and AI.

6. A real-world example of autonomous system troubleshooting developed by Dell Technologies.

7. The era in which quantum computing and AI will dominate the technology landscape.

8. A technology that will integrate troubleshooting into cloud ecosystems for remote diagnostics.

9. The method used by Google to develop AI-powered conversational troubleshooting.

10. The expected impact of quantum-enhanced AI tools on future troubleshooting systems.

Test III: True-or-False Questions

Instructions: Read each statement carefully. Write T if the statement is true and F if it is false.

1. Self-healing systems require continuous human intervention to fix issues.

2. Quantum computing diagnostics are already widely used in consumer devices.

3. Collaborative AI platforms will reduce the need for human involvement in troubleshooting.

4. Troubleshooting in 2030 will likely involve virtual reality interfaces for interacting with hardware models.

5. AI tools are expected to become less accurate and reliable by 2030.

6. IBM's educational programs focus on preparing professionals for quantum computing and AI advancements.

7. Self-healing systems in PCs are expected to automatically repair corruption without user input.

8. Virtual reality interfaces are predicted to play no role in future troubleshooting.

9. The integration of AI in troubleshooting systems will reduce the need for cloud technologies.

10. Quantum-enhanced AI tools will offer more precise diagnostic capabilities than current systems.

Test IV: Matching-Type Questions

Instructions: Match the items in Column A with their corresponding descriptions in Column B. Write the letter of the correct match on the blank provided.

Column A

1. Self-Healing Systems

2. Quantum Computing Diagnostics

3. Collaborative AI Platforms

4. Virtual Reality Troubleshooting

5. 2030 Troubleshooting Predictions

6. Quantum-Enhanced AI Tools

7. IBM's Educational Programs

8. AI-Driven Diagnostic Tools

9. Google's AI Advances

10. Cloud-Based Remote Diagnostics

Column B

A. Tools allowing multiple AI technologies to work together for efficient problem resolution.

B. Training programs preparing professionals for quantum computing and AI.

C. Predictive tools that autonomously diagnose and repair issues without human intervention.

D. Expected method for interacting with hardware models in 2030 troubleshooting.

E. Offers unmatched diagnostic precision, integrating quantum computing.

F. The ability of PCs to automatically fix problems without external intervention.

G. Remote diagnostics for efficient troubleshooting using cloud infrastructure.

H. Developments in AI allowing natural language troubleshooting conversations.

I. Technology enabling troubleshooting and diagnostics for quantum systems.

J. Future systems involving seamless integration with virtual reality and AI technologies.

Test V: Essay Question

Instructions: Write a concise and well-organized essay on the following topic. Provide specific examples to support your answer.

Question:

Discuss the role of emerging technologies such as self-healing systems, quantum computing diagnostics, and collaborative AI platforms in shaping the future of PC troubleshooting. How will these innovations impact the efficiency and accuracy of troubleshooting processes by 2030?

Final Thoughts

As we stand on the cusp of transformative advancements in computing, the ability to troubleshoot and optimize PC systems has never been more essential. The innovations discussed in this book—from AI-driven diagnostics to quantum computing—represent not just the future of technology but also opportunities for individuals and businesses to thrive in an increasingly interconnected world.

Embracing these changes requires adaptability, curiosity, and a commitment to continuous learning. Whether you are a seasoned professional or a newcomer to the field, the skills and knowledge outlined in this book will serve as your foundation for navigating the ever-evolving technological landscape.

Thank you for embarking on this journey with me. Here's to mastering the challenges and seizing the opportunities that the future of PC troubleshooting holds.

Glossary

Artificial Intelligence (AI): The simulation of human intelligence processes by machines, especially computer systems, to perform tasks such as learning, reasoning, and problem-solving.

BIOS (Basic Input/Output System): Firmware used to perform hardware initialization during the booting process and to provide runtime services for operating systems and programs.

Cloud Computing: The delivery of computing services—including servers, storage, databases, networking, software, and analytics—over the internet ("the cloud") to offer faster innovation and flexible resources.

Containerization: A lightweight form of virtualization that packages software code and its dependencies together to ensure it runs uniformly across different environments.

Quantum Computing: A type of computing that uses quantum-mechanical phenomena, such as superposition and entanglement, to perform calculations at speeds significantly faster than traditional computers.

Troubleshooting: The systematic process of diagnosing and resolving problems or malfunctions in hardware or software systems.

UEFI (Unified Extensible Firmware Interface): A modern version of BIOS that provides additional features and faster boot times for computers.

References

1. American Psychological Association (APA) 7th Edition Style

2. Evans, J. R., & Lindsay, W. M. (2020). Managing for quality and performance excellence (11th ed.). Cengage Learning.

3. IBM Quantum. (n.d.). IBM quantum experience. Retrieved from https://www.ibm.com/quantum-computing/

4. NVIDIA. (2023). GeForce now: Cloud gaming. Retrieved from https://www.nvidia.com/en-us/geforce-now/

5. Microsoft Corporation. (2023). Windows 12: Features and updates. Retrieved from https://www.microsoft.com/windows12

6. Canonical. (2023). Ubuntu for enterprise computing. Retrieved from https://ubuntu.com/

7. Lenovo. (2023). Predictive analytics in system maintenance. Retrieved from https://www.lenovo.com

8. AMD. (2023). Zen 5 architecture: Advancements and benefits. Retrieved from https://www.amd.com

9. Google AI. (2023). Conversational AI for diagnostics. Retrieved from https://ai.google/

10. Dell Technologies. (2023). Self-healing systems for enterprise computing. Retrieved from https://www.dell.com

11. Helium Network. (2023). Blockchain-powered IoT networks. Retrieved from https://www.helium.com

About The Author

Early Life and Education

Mark John Lado was born on September 24, 1992, in Danao City,

Philippines. From an early age, he exhibited a keen interest in technology and education, which would later shape his career. He pursued his Bachelor of Science in Information Systems (BSIS) at Colegio de San Antonio de Padua, where he graduated with a strong foundation in technology and systems analysis. His academic journey continued as he earned a Master's degree in Information Technology (MIT) from the Northern Negros State College of Science and Technology in Sagay City, Philippines. Currently, he is pursuing his Doctorate in Information Technology at the State University of Northern Negros, reflecting his commitment to lifelong learning and professional growth.

Professional Career

Mark has built a diverse and impactful career in education and technology. He currently serves as an Instructor in the College of Technology and Engineering at Cebu Technological University, a role he has held since October 2022. Prior to this, he was a Faculty member in Business Education and Information Systems at Colegio de San Antonio de Padua from 2018 to 2022. His earlier roles include working as a Part-Time Information Technology Instructor at the University of the Visayas - Danao Branch and as an ICT Coordinator at Carmen Christian School Inc. in 2017.

Research and Innovation

Mark is an active researcher with a focus on applying technology to solve real-world problems. Some of his notable projects include:

1. "Development of a Microprocessor-Based Sensor Network for Monitoring Water Parameters in Tilapia Traponds"

2. "A Wireless Digital Public Address with Voice Alarm and Text-to-Speech Feature for Different Campuses", which was published in Globus: An International Journal of Management & IT

His research contributions highlight his dedication to innovation and his ability to bridge theoretical knowledge with practical applications.

Authorship and Publications

Mark is a prolific author, having written and published multiple books on technology topics. His works include:

1. Mastering CRUD with Flask in 5 Days; Build Python Web Applications - From Novice to...

2. Flask, PostgreSQL, and Bootstrap: Building Data-Driven Web Applications with CRUD...

3. From Model to Web App: A Comprehensive Guide to Building Data-Driven Web...

4. The Beginner's Guide Computer Systems; Principles, Practices, and Troubleshooting:...

5. Flask Web Framework Building Interactive Web Applications with SQLite Database: A...

6. Mastering PC Troubleshooting & Operating Systems: The Modern Landscape of PC...

7. Mastering Flask in 5 Days; From Zero to Deployment: Building Your First Web App:...

8. Data Modeling and Process Analysis; Essential for Technology Analysts and AI...

9. The Echo of the Past; Information Networks from Stone to Silicon and Beyond AI: How...

10. Cybersecurity Essentials Protecting Your Digital Life, Data, and Privacy in a...

11. Mastering PC Troubleshooting and Operating Systems: The Future-Ready...

12. From Idea to Manuscript: A Step-by-Step Guide to Writing Your Nonfiction Book

13. Microprocessor Magic: Unlocking the Potential of Building Projects from Scratch

14. Data Modeling and Process Analysis: A Comprehensive Guide – Volume I

15. Python Data Science Essentials: A Comprehensive Guide to Mastering...

16. Mastering PC Troubleshooting and Operating Systems: A Comprehensive Guide

17. Cybersecurity Confidence: 8 Steps to Master Digital Security and Boost Productivity

18. Embedded Systems: From Historical Development to Modern-Day Applications

These books are widely recognized and serve as valuable resources for students, hobbyists, and professionals in the IT field. His publications are available on platforms like Amazon and ThriftBooks, further extending his reach and impact

Certifications and Professional Development

Mark has pursued several certifications to enhance his expertise, including:

- Computer Hardware Servicing from Cebu Technological University

- Consumer Electronics Servicing from TESDA

These certifications underscore his commitment to continuous professional development and staying updated with emerging technological trends.

Contributions to IT Education

As an active member of the Philippine Society of Information Technology Educators (PSITE), Mark contributes to advancing IT education standards in the Philippines. His teaching, research, and authorship have made him a respected figure in the academic and IT communities. He is known for his adaptability to emerging technologies, such as AI-driven systems and cybersecurity, ensuring that his work remains relevant and impactful.

Personal Interests

Outside of his professional life, Mark enjoys reading books, spending time at the beach, and engaging in physical activities like inline skating and biking. These hobbies not only help him unwind but also contribute to his overall well-being and creativity.

Legacy and Impact

Mark John Lado's dedication to education, research, and professional excellence has made him a valuable asset to the IT community. His contributions have empowered countless students and professionals, preparing them for the challenges of a rapidly evolving technological landscape. His unwavering passion for technology and continuous pursuit of learning ensure that his legacy will endure for years to come.

For more details about his work, you can visit his official website https://markjohnlado.com/

or explore his publications on Amazon Author Page

https://www.amazon.com/stores/author/B0BZM8PM6R

I highly recommend reading this book to further enhance your skills and deepen your understanding of the subject.

https://a.co/d/ahv6VWa

https://a.co/d/b1W3F8n

https://a.co/d/izTWNbO

https://a.co/d/6HHyUFk

www.ingramcontent.com/pod-product-compliance
Lightning Source LLC
Chambersburg PA
CBHW071004050326
40689CB00014B/3489